contents

Please note that Australian cup and
spoon measurements are metric.
A conversion chart appears on page 62.

banana split

4 medium bananas (800g), halved lengthways
2 tablespoons brown sugar
100g dark eating chocolate
300ml thickened cream
1 tablespoon dark rum
4 scoops (240ml) vanilla ice-cream
4 scoops (240ml) chocolate ice-cream
⅔ cup (80g) coarsely chopped roasted pecans
⅓ cup (25g) toasted shredded coconut

1 Preheat grill.
2 Place bananas, cut-sides up, on oven tray; sprinkle with sugar. Grill about 3 minutes or until sugar melts.
3 Meanwhile, melt chocolate with 2 tablespoons of the cream in small bowl set over small saucepan of simmering water (do not let water touch base of bowl).
4 Beat remaining cream with rum in small bowl with electric mixer until soft peaks form.
5 Place 2 banana halves in each of four dishes; top each with a scoop of the vanilla and chocolate ice-cream then drizzle with chocolate. Top with cream and sprinkle with nuts and coconut.

preparation time 20 minutes
cooking time 10 minutes
serves 4

quick mango ice-cream

You will need three medium (1.3kg) mangoes for this recipe.

2 cups (500ml) mango puree
½ cup (125ml) thickened cream
1½ cups (375ml) ready-made custard
¼ cup (60ml) lemon juice
½ cup (80g) icing sugar

1 Combine ingredients in large bowl; pour into ice-cream maker. Churn according to manufacturer's directions. (Or, pour mixture into a loaf pan, cover with foil and freeze until a 2cm rim has formed around the edge. Transfer mixture to chilled bowl; beat with electric mixer until all ice particles have broken up. Return to pan; freeze until almost firm.) Chop and beat once more.
2 Pour mixture into loaf pan, cover with foil and freeze until firm.

preparation time 10 minutes (plus freezing time)
makes 1 litre

raspberry vanilla ice-cream sandwiches

125g strawberries, sliced thickly
2 teaspoons caster sugar
2 scoops raspberry sorbet
6 Lattice biscuits
2 scoops vanilla ice-cream
100g raspberries

1 Combine strawberries and sugar in small bowl.
2 Sandwich sorbet between two biscuits on each serving plate, top with ice-cream and remaining biscuits.
3 Add raspberries to strawberry mixture. Serve ice-cream sandwiches with berry mixture.

preparation time 10 minutes
serves 2

affogato with frangelico

⅓ cup ground espresso coffee
1½ cups (375ml) boiling water
1 litre good-quality vanilla ice-cream
½ cup (125ml) Frangelico

1 Place coffee in coffee plunger, add water; stand 4 minutes before plunging.
2 Divide ice-cream among six heatproof serving glasses; pour 1 tablespoon liqueur over ice-cream in each glass.
3 Give hot coffee to guests to pour over the ice-cream.

preparation time 10 minutes
serves 6
notes Pour your favourite liqueur over the ice-cream; orange and or chocolate flavours work well with the coffee.
Use a good-quality french vanilla or panna cotta ice-cream.

vanilla bean ice-cream

2 vanilla beans
1⅔ cups (410ml) milk
600ml thickened cream
8 egg yolks
¾ cup (165g) caster sugar

1 Split vanilla beans lengthways; scrape out seeds into medium saucepan. Add pods, milk and cream; bring mixture almost to the boil. Remove milk mixture from heat; discard vanilla bean.
2 Meanwhile, whisk egg yolks and sugar in medium bowl until creamy. Whisking constantly, gradually pour milk mixture into egg mixture. Return custard mixture to same pan; cook over low heat, stirring constantly, until mixture begins to thicken and coats the back of a spoon (do not boil or mixture will curdle).
3 Strain mixture into medium heatproof bowl. Cover surface of custard with plastic wrap; refrigerate about 1 hour or until cold.
4 Pour custard into ice-cream maker, churn according to manufacturer's instructions. (Or place custard in shallow container, such as an aluminium slab cake pan, cover with foil; freeze until almost firm.) Place ice-cream in large bowl, chop coarsely then beat with electric mixer until smooth. Pour into deep container, cover; freeze until firm. Repeat process two more times.

preparation time 15 minutes (plus refrigeration and freezing time)
cooking time 10 minutes
serves 8
tip Store ice-cream in freezer, covered, for up to four weeks.

lemon bombes alaska

2¾ cups (680ml) slightly
  softened vanilla ice-cream
30g unsalted butter
½ teaspoon finely grated
  lemon rind
1 tablespoon lemon juice
1 egg yolk
¼ cup (55g) caster sugar
⅓ cup (80ml) limoncello
½ cup (125ml) thickened
  cream
290g bought sponge cake
2 egg whites
⅓ cup (75g) caster sugar,
  extra

preparation time 40 minutes
(plus refrigeration time)
cooking time 20 minutes
serves 4
tip Bombes can be prepared
the day before serving to the
stage at which they are ready
to be baked; freeze until ready
to bake.

1 Line four ½-cup (125ml) moulds with plastic
wrap. Press ⅓ cup ice-cream firmly up and
around inside of each mould to form cavity.
Cover with foil; freeze 2 hours. Return remaining
ice-cream to freezer.

2 Combine butter, rind, juice, yolk and sugar in
small heatproof bowl; stir over small saucepan
of simmering water until mixture thickens slightly.
Stir in liqueur. Cover surface of lemon curd with
plastic wrap; refrigerate until cold.

3 Place 1 tablespoon of the lemon curd into
each mould, cover; freeze until firm. Combine
remaining lemon curd with cream, cover;
refrigerate lemon cream until serving.

4 Remove moulds from the freezer, spread
enough remaining ice-cream over lemon curd
to fill moulds; cover, freeze bombes until firm.

5 Preheat oven to 240°C/220°C fan-forced.

6 Cut four rounds from sponge cake, large
enough to cover top of each mould.

7 Beat egg whites in small bowl with electric
mixer until soft peaks form; add extra sugar,
1 tablespoon at a time, beating until sugar
dissolves between additions.

8 Turn one bombe onto one round of sponge
cake on oven tray; peel away plastic wrap.
Spread a quarter of the meringue mixture over
to enclose bombe completely; repeat to make
a total of four bombes.

9 Bake bombes, uncovered, about 3 minutes
or until browned lightly. Serve immediately with
lemon cream.

pineapple ice

1 large pineapple (2kg), chopped coarsely
¾ cup (165g) caster sugar
2 cups (500ml) water
¼ cup finely chopped fresh mint
4 egg whites

1 Blend or process pineapple until smooth; push through sieve
into medium bowl. Discard pulp.
2 Combine sugar and the water in medium saucepan; stir over
low heat until sugar dissolves. Bring to the boil; reduce heat.
Simmer, uncovered, without stirring, about 10 minutes or until
syrup thickens slightly. Cool then stir in mint.
3 Stir syrup into pineapple juice, cover with foil; freeze about
3 hours or until just set.
4 Remove mixture from freezer; using fork, scrape mixture to
break up then place in large bowl with egg whites. Beat with
electric mixer until smooth.
5 Pour mixture into 19cm x 29cm lamington pan, cover with
foil; freeze overnight (stir occasionally while freezing to distribute
mixture evenly).
6 Serve pineapple ice with slices of extra fresh pineapple,
if you like.

preparation time 30 minutes (plus cooling and freezing time)
cooking time 10 minutes
serves 6

cherry white chocolate ice-cream

¾ cup (180ml) water
1 cup (220g) caster sugar
500g cherries,
    stones removed
2 tablespoons vodka, optional
    (see note, below)
1 tablespoon caster sugar,
    extra
1 litre vanilla ice-cream
100g white eating chocolate,
    chopped finely
½ cup (75g) vienna almonds,
    chopped finely

1 Combine water and sugar in medium saucepan; stir over low heat until sugar dissolves. Add cherries; bring to the boil. Reduce heat; simmer, covered, about 10 minutes or until cherries are tender. Using a slotted spoon, transfer cherries to a bowl. Boil cherry liquid, uncovered, about 10 minutes or until syrup thickens slightly.
2 Meanwhile, coarsely chop half the cherries. Combine chopped cherries in small bowl with vodka and extra sugar; stand 10 minutes. Drain, discard liquid.
3 Remove ice-cream from freezer; stand 10 minutes or until softened slightly. Transfer to large bowl; gently fold in chopped cherries, chocolate and almonds.
4 Line 14cm x 21cm loaf pan with plastic wrap. Spread mixture into pan; cover, freeze overnight.
5 Wipe base and sides of pan with a warm cloth; turn ice-cream out onto serving plate.
6 Slice ice-cream; serve with remaining cherries and syrup.

preparation time 15 minutes
(plus freezing time)
cooking time 25 minutes
serves 6
note The vodka will help to prevent the cherries becoming too hard and icy when frozen. You can omit it, if preferred.

ginger and almond biscotti ice-cream sandwiches

3 egg whites
½ cup (110g) caster sugar
1 teaspoon vanilla extract
¾ cup (110g) plain flour
¼ cup (30g) almond meal
2 tablespoons finely chopped crystallised ginger
¼ cup (40g) roasted blanched almonds
⅔ cup (160ml) ice-cream

1 Preheat oven to 180°C/160°C fan-forced. Lightly grease 8cm x 25cm bar cake pan; line base and long sides with baking paper, extending paper 5cm over sides of pan.

2 Beat egg whites in small bowl with electric mixer until soft peaks form. With motor operating, gradually add sugar, beating until sugar dissolves. Beat in extract then fold in sifted flour, almond meal, ginger and nuts.

3 Spread mixture into prepared pan; bake, uncovered, about 25 minutes or until firm. Turn oven off. Remove pan from oven and cool loaf to room temperature in pan. Cover; refrigerate 2 hours.

4 Preheat oven to 160°C/140°C fan-forced. Line oven tray with baking paper. Trim brown sides from loaf then slice into 16 pieces.

5 Place pieces on oven tray; bake, uncovered, about 20 minutes or until biscotti are crisp and browned lightly. Cool on tray. Sandwich ice-cream between biscotti.

preparation time 25 minutes
(plus cooling and refrigeration time)
cooking time 45 minutes
makes 8
note Biscotti can be made up to a week ahead and kept in an airtight container.

green apple frozen yogurt

You need to buy one green apple weighing about 275g for this recipe.

⅓ cup (115g) honey
½ cup (125ml) apple juice
1 teaspoon gelatine
¾ cup (130g) finely grated
  unpeeled apple
500g greek-style yogurt
1 tablespoon passionfruit pulp

1 Stir honey and juice in small saucepan over low heat until honey melts; cool syrup 5 minutes.
2 Sprinkle gelatine over syrup; stir until gelatine dissolves.
3 Combine gelatine mixture, apple and yogurt in 14cm x 21cm loaf pan. Cover with foil; freeze 3 hours or overnight. Remove yogurt from freezer 15 minutes before serving. Divide yogurt among serving glasses; top each with 1 teaspoon of pulp.

preparation time 15 minutes
(plus freezing time)
cooking time 5 minutes
serves 4

variations
raspberry
Substitute water for the juice in step 1; substitute 150g thawed frozen raspberries for the apple. Push thawed raspberries through a fine sieve over small bowl; discard seeds.

mango
Substitute water for the juice in step 1; substitute 300g thawed coarsely chopped frozen mango for the apple.

peanut butter and fudge ice-cream pie

300g packet chocolate chip
  cookies
40g butter, melted
1 tablespoon milk
1 litre good-quality vanilla
  ice-cream, softened slightly
1⅓ cups (375g) crunchy
  peanut butter
hot fudge sauce
200g dark eating chocolate,
  chopped coarsely
50g white marshmallows,
  chopped coarsely
300ml thickened cream

1 Grease 24cm-round loose-based flan tin.
2 Blend or process cookies until mixture resembles coarse breadcrumbs. Add butter and milk; process until combined.
3 Press cookie mixture evenly over base and around side of prepared tin; refrigerate 10 minutes.
4 Beat softened ice-cream and peanut butter in large bowl with electric mixer until combined. Spoon filling into crumb crust. Cover; freeze pie 3 hours or overnight.
5 Make hot fudge sauce.
6 Drizzle slices of pie with sauce to serve.
hot fudge sauce Combine ingredients in small saucepan; stir over heat, without boiling, until smooth.

preparation time 20 minutes
(plus freezing time)
cooking time 10 minutes
serves 10
notes Warm a large knife under hot water, quickly dry it and cut the pie while the knife is still hot.
Marshmallows come in many sizes and colours; the largest white type is best for this recipe.

brownie ice-cream stacks with hot mocha fudge sauce

500ml vanilla ice-cream,
   softened slightly
80g butter
150g dark eating chocolate,
   chopped coarsely
¾ cup (150g) firmly packed
   brown sugar
2 eggs, beaten lightly
½ cup (75g) plain flour
¼ cup (60g) sour cream
½ cup (50g) coarsely chopped
   walnuts
hot mocha fudge sauce
50g dark eating chocolate,
   chopped coarsely
½ cup (125ml) cream
2 tablespoons brown sugar
½ teaspoon instant
   coffee granules
1 tablespoon coffee-flavoured
   liqueur

1 Line base and sides of 8cm x 26cm bar cake pan with baking paper. Press ice-cream into pan, cover with foil; freeze overnight.
2 Preheat oven to 180C/160°C fan-forced. Line base and sides of another 8cm x 26cm bar cake pan with baking paper.
3 Combine butter and chocolate in small saucepan; stir over low heat until mixture is smooth. Transfer chocolate mixture to medium bowl. Stir in sugar; cool.
4 Stir eggs then sifted flour, sour cream and nuts into chocolate mixture. Spread mixture into prepared pan; bake, uncovered, in oven about 40 minutes. Cool brownie in pan.
5 Meanwhile, make hot mocha fudge sauce.
6 Turn brownie onto wire rack; remove paper. Trim narrow ends; cut brownie into 12 slices.
7 Turn ice-cream out of pan; cut into eight slices. Stack alternate slices of ice-cream and brownie starting and finishing with brownie. Drizzle each stack with hot mocha fudge sauce.
hot mocha fudge sauce Combine chocolate, cream, sugar and coffee in small saucepan. Stir over low heat until mixture is smooth; bring to the boil. Reduce heat; simmer, uncovered, 2 minutes. Remove from heat; stir in liqueur.

preparation time 20 minutes
(plus freezing time)
cooking time 45 minutes
serves 4

watermelon and mint granita

You need half a large seedless watermelon (about 3kg) to get the amount of chopped watermelon needed for this recipe.

2 cups (500ml) water
1 cup (220g) white sugar
1.6kg coarsely chopped watermelon
2 cups firmly packed fresh mint leaves

1 Combine the water and sugar in medium saucepan. Stir over low heat, without boiling, until sugar dissolves; bring to the boil. Reduce heat; simmer, uncovered, without stirring, about 5 minutes or until syrup thickens slightly but does not colour.
2 Blend or process watermelon and mint, in batches, until almost smooth; push batches through sieve into large bowl. Add syrup; stir to combine.
3 Pour mixture into two 20cm x 30cm lamington pans, cover with foil; freeze about 3 hours or until almost set.
4 Using fork, scrape granita from bottom and sides of pans, mixing frozen with unfrozen mixture. Cover, return to freezer. Repeat process every hour for about 4 hours or until large ice crystals form and granita has a dry, shard-like appearance. Scrape again with fork before serving.

preparation time 10 minutes (plus freezing time)
cooking time 10 minutes
serves 8

mango frozen yogurt

3 egg yolks
⅔ cup (150g) caster sugar
300ml cream
1¼ cups (310ml) milk
1¾ cups (500g) greek-style yogurt
2 small ripe mangoes (600g), peeled, chopped coarsely

1 Whisk egg yolks and sugar in medium bowl until light and fluffy.
2 Bring cream and milk almost to the boil in medium saucepan. Remove from heat. Whisking constantly, gradually pour cream mixture into egg mixture.
3 Return custard mixture to pan; cook over low heat, stirring constantly, until mixture thickens and coats the back of a spoon. Do not boil.
4 Transfer mixture to large bowl; cover, refrigerate until cold.
5 Stir yogurt into cold custard. Churn mixture in an ice-cream maker, following manufacturer's instructions, until beginning to thicken (or see note, below). Add mangoes, churn until firm.
6 Transfer mixture to 1.5-litre (6-cup) freezer-proof container. Cover; freeze about 4 hours or until firm.
7 Serve scooped in glasses with extra sliced mango, if desired.

preparation time 25 minutes
cooking time 10 minutes (plus refrigeration and freezing time)
makes 1.5 litres (6 cups)
tip Without an electric ice-cream maker, freeze mixture until partially frozen; chop coarsely then beat with an electric mixer until smooth. Fold in chopped mango; freeze until firm. Store frozen yogurt, covered, in freezer for up to three months.

chocolate ice-cream with toffee-brittle

230g peanut brittle
1 litre good-quality ice-cream
100g dark eating chocolate, shaved

1   Refrigerate peanut brittle until ready to serve dessert. Put brittle into a
strong plastic bag and coarsely crush with a meat mallet or small hammer.
2   Divide scoops of ice-cream among six serving dishes; sprinkle over
crushed brittle then shaved chocolate.

preparation time 10 minutes
serves 6

vanilla bean ice-cream with choc-almond crunch

2 egg yolks
⅓ cup (75g) caster sugar
1 cup (250ml) milk
300ml thickened cream
1 vanilla bean, halved
   lengthways
choc-almond crunch
2 cups (440g) caster sugar
1 cup (250ml) water
200g dark eating chocolate,
   chopped coarsely
½ cup (40g) flaked almonds,
   roasted

preparation time 20 minutes
(plus refrigeration time)
cooking time 20 minutes
serves 6
tip Milk chocolate can be
used instead of dark eating
chocolate, if preferred.

1 Whisk egg yolks and sugar in medium bowl until light and fluffy.

2 Combine milk and cream in medium saucepan. Scrape seeds from vanilla bean. Add bean and seeds to pan; bring milk mixture almost to the boil.

3 Remove milk mixture from heat; discard vanilla bean. Whisking constantly, gradually pour milk mixture into egg mixture. Return custard mixture to same pan; cook over low heat, stirring constantly, until mixture begins to thicken and coats the back of a spoon (do not boil or mixture will curdle).

4 Return custard to same medium bowl. Cover surface completely with plastic wrap; freeze about 4 hours or until ice-cream is firm.

5 Make choc-almond crunch.

6 Line 8cm x 25cm bar cake pan with plastic wrap. Blend or process ice-cream until smooth; spread into prepared pan. Cover with foil; freeze until firm. Turn ice-cream out of pan; cut bar into 12 slices. Serve with choc-almond crunch.

choc-almond crunch Combine sugar and the water in medium heavy-based saucepan; stir over low heat until sugar dissolves. Increase heat; bring to the boil. Boil, uncovered, without stirring, about 10 minutes or until syrup is a deep golden colour. Pour toffee mixture into 20cm x 30cm lamington pan; stand 5 minutes. Sprinkle chocolate over hot toffee, spreading with palette knife to completely cover toffee. Sprinkle with nuts; refrigerate until set. Break choc-almond crunch into shards.

pineapple and mint ice-blocks

1½ cups (375ml) pineapple juice
2 tablespoons icing sugar
2 teaspoons finely chopped fresh mint

1   Combine ingredients in medium jug. Pour mixture into six ¼ cup (60ml) ice-block moulds. Press lids on firmly; freeze 6 hours or overnight.

preparation time 5 minutes (plus freezing time)
makes 6
note   To remove ice-blocks from moulds, dip into hot water for a few seconds, loosen lids and squeeze sides of moulds – the ice-blocks should slide out easily. If you like, insert ice-block sticks into ice-blocks before freezing.

honey buttermilk ice-cream with fresh fruit salsa

2 teaspoons gelatine
¼ cup (60ml) water
1½ cups (375ml) low-fat
  evaporated milk
½ cup (175g) honey
1½ cups (375ml) buttermilk
fresh fruit salsa
1 small pineapple (800g),
  chopped coarsely
1 large mango (600g),
  chopped coarsely
3 medium kiwifruit (255g),
  chopped coarsely
250g strawberries,
  chopped coarsely

1 Sprinkle gelatine over the water in small heatproof jug; stand jug in pan of simmering water. Stir until gelatine dissolves; cool.

2 Meanwhile, place evaporated milk in medium saucepan; bring to the boil. Remove from heat; stir in gelatine mixture and honey. Transfer to medium bowl; cool.

3 Beat buttermilk in small bowl with electric mixer until buttermilk is frothy.

4 Beat evaporated milk mixture with electric mixer until light and frothy. With motor operating, gradually pour in buttermilk; beat until combined.

5 Pour into 2-litre (8-cup) metal container. Cover with foil; freeze about 3 hours or until just set.

6 Beat ice-cream with electric mixer until smooth. Re-cover with foil; freeze overnight or until set.

7 Make fresh fruit salsa, serve with ice-cream.

fruit salsa Combine fruit in medium bowl.

preparation time 30 minutes
(plus freezing time)
cooking time 10 minutes
serves 6
note The ice-cream can also be made in an ice-cream maker; pour the mixture into the ice-cream maker in step 5 and follow the manufacturer's instructions.

ice-cream sundae with berry sauce and almond wafers

⅓ cup (75g) firmly packed
  brown sugar
25g butter
½ cup (125ml) thickened cream
1 cup (150g) frozen mixed
  berries
500ml vanilla ice-cream
500ml strawberry ice-cream
almond wafers
1 egg white
2 tablespoons caster sugar
2 tablespoons plain flour
20g butter, melted
2 tablespoons flaked almonds

1   Make almond wafers.

2   Combine sugar, butter and cream in small saucepan; bring to the boil. Reduce heat; simmer, uncovered, stirring, about 5 minutes or until slightly thickened. Remove from heat; stir in berries.

3   Divide both ice-creams among four 1½-cup (375ml) serving glasses; drizzle with berry sauce. Serve with almond wafers.

almond wafers Preheat oven to 180°C/160°C fan-forced. Lightly grease two oven trays. Beat egg white in small bowl with electric mixer until soft peaks form. Gradually add sugar, beating until dissolved after each addition; fold in sifted flour and butter. Drop rounded teaspoons of mixture 10cm apart on greased oven trays (approximately four per tray); sprinkle with nuts. Bake, uncovered, about 5 minutes or until wafers are browned lightly; cool on trays.

preparation time 20 minutes
cooking time 10 minutes
serves 4

chocolate, nut and coffee ice-cream cake

Vienna almonds are toffee-coated almonds available from selected supermarkets, nut stands and gourmet food and specialty confectionery stores. Crème de cacao is a chocolate-flavoured liqueur and can be found in most liquor stores.

2 litres good-quality
  vanilla ice-cream
1 tablespoon instant coffee
  granules
1 tablespoon hot water
½ cup (70g) vienna almonds,
  chopped coarsely
100g dark eating chocolate,
  melted
1 tablespoon crème de cacao
100g white eating chocolate,
  melted
½ cup (75g) roasted pistachios,
  chopped coarsely

notes It is important each layer sets firm before adding the next.
To remove ice-cream cake easily, rub sides of tin with a hot cloth.

1 Grease 21cm springform tin; line base and side with baking paper.
2 Divide ice-cream into three portions; return two portions to freezer. Soften remaining ice-cream in medium bowl.
3 Dissolve coffee in the water in small jug, cool; stir into softened ice-cream with two-thirds of the almonds. Spoon into prepared tin, cover; freeze about 2 hours or until firm.
4 Soften second portion of ice-cream in medium bowl; stir in dark eating chocolate. Microwave, uncovered, on MEDIUM-HIGH (80%) about 2 minutes or until chocolate melts; whisk until smooth. Stir in liqueur, cover; freeze about 1 hour or until almost firm. Spoon dark chocolate ice-cream over coffee layer, cover; freeze about 2 hours or until firm.
5 Soften remaining ice-cream in medium bowl; fold in white chocolate. Microwave, uncovered, on MEDIUM-HIGH (80%) about 2 minutes or until chocolate melts; whisk until smooth. Stir in two-thirds of the pistachios, cover; freeze about 1 hour or until almost firm, stirring ice-cream occasionally to suspend pistachios evenly. Spoon white chocolate ice-cream over dark chocolate layer, cover; freeze about 2 hours or until firm.
6 Remove ice-cream cake from tin just before serving; sprinkle with remaining nuts.

preparation time 35 minutes
(plus freezing time)
serves 10

banana caramel sundae

70g dark eating chocolate, chopped finely
⅔ cup (70g) roasted walnuts, chopped coarsely
1 litre vanilla ice-cream
4 medium bananas (800g), chopped coarsely
caramel sauce
100g butter
½ cup (125ml) cream
½ cup (110g) firmly packed brown sugar

1 Make caramel sauce.
2 Divide one-third of the sauce among six ¾-cup (180ml) glasses;
divide half the chocolate, nuts, ice-cream and banana among glasses.
Repeat layering process, ending with a layer of the sauce.
caramel sauce Combine ingredients in small saucepan. Stir over
low heat until sugar dissolves; bring to the boil. Reduce heat; simmer,
uncovered, 5 minutes. Cool.

preparation time 10 minutes
cooking time 10 minutes
serves 6

raspberry rapture ice-cream cakes

500ml raspberry ice-cream, softened
180g white eating chocolate, melted
pink food colouring
450g store-bought madeira cake
¼ cup (80g) raspberry jam

1 Grease 15cm x 25cm loaf pan; line with baking paper, extending paper 5cm over long sides.
2 Spread ice-cream into pan, cover with foil; freeze until firm.
3 Remove ice-cream from pan. Cut six 6.5cm hearts from ice-cream; place hearts on baking-paper-lined tray, cover with foil; freeze until firm.
4 Line another tray with baking paper. Tint melted chocolate pink with food colouring. Spread chocolate over baking paper on tray into 22cm x 30cm rectangle; stand at room temperature about 5 minutes or until almost set. Cut 12 x 6.5cm hearts from chocolate. Return to tray; refrigerate until set.
5 Meanwhile, freeze cake until firm. Slice cake into 12 x 1cm-thick slices. Cut one 6.5cm heart from each slice.
6 Spread one side of all cakes with jam; top with chocolate hearts. Sandwich plain sides of cakes with ice-cream hearts. Serve immediately or return to freezer until required.

preparation time 25 minutes (plus freezing and standing time)
makes 6

chocolate hazelnut ice-cream cones

1 litre good-quality vanilla ice-cream
⅓ cup (100g) chocolate hazelnut spread
6 Baci chocolates, chopped coarsely
6 waffle ice-cream cones

1 Soften ice-cream in large bowl; stir in spread and chocolate.
2 Pour mixture into loaf pan; cover and freeze overnight or until firm.
3 Scoop ice-cream and serve in cones.

preparation time 10 minutes (plus freezing time)
makes 6
notes This recipe can be made a week ahead.
Meaning "kisses" in Italian, Baci chocolates have a rich hazelnut centre
covered in a creamy dark chocolate coating and wrapped in a poetic love
note. Use any chocolate-covered hazelnut chocolate you like.

mango vanilla frozen yogurt swirls

You will need two medium mangoes (860g) for this recipe.

1⅓ cups (330ml) mango puree
⅓ cup (55g) icing sugar
1⅓ cups (375g) greek-style yogurt
1 teaspoon vanilla bean paste (or vanilla extract)

1 Combine puree, 1 tablespoon of the sifted icing sugar and 2 tablespoons of the yogurt in small bowl.
2 Combine remaining sifted icing sugar, yogurt and vanilla paste in another small bowl.
3 Spoon a third of the mango mixture into eight ⅓-cup (80ml) ice-block moulds. Top with half the yogurt mixture; swirl with a skewer. Repeat with remaining mango and yogurt mixtures.
4 Press lids firmly on ice-block moulds, insert ice-block sticks if desired. Freeze 6 hours or overnight.

preparation time 25 minutes (plus freezing time)
serves 8

lemon sorbet

You need four lemons for this recipe.

2½ cups (625ml) water
¼ cup finely grated lemon rind
1 cup (220g) caster sugar
¾ cup (180ml) lemon juice
1 egg white

1 Stir the water, rind and sugar in small saucepan over heat, without boiling, until sugar dissolves; bring to the boil. Boil, uncovered, without stirring, about 5 minutes or until syrup thickens slightly. Strain into medium heatproof jug; cool to room temperature. Stir in juice.
2 Pour sorbet mixture into 14cm x 21cm loaf pan, cover with foil; freeze about 3 hours or until almost set.
3 Blend or process mixture with egg white until smooth. Return to pan, cover; freeze 3 hours or overnight.

preparation time 15 minutes (plus cooling and freezing time)
cooking time 10 minutes
serves 4
note You can also freeze the sorbet-egg white mixture in an ice-cream machine following the manufacturer's instructions (see step 2).

chocolate honeycomb ice-cream towers

2 cups (500ml) milk
300ml cream
5 egg yolks
½ cup (110g) caster sugar
1 tablespoon custard powder
100g dark eating chocolate,
    chopped finely
¼ cup (60ml) coffee-flavoured
    liqueur
50g chocolate honeycomb
    bars, chopped coarsely
1⅓ cups (200g) dark
    chocolate Melts, melted

1   Grease six ¾-cup (180ml) dishes; line with plastic wrap, bringing wrap 5cm over sides. Freeze until ready to use.

2   Combine milk and cream in medium saucepan, bring to the boil. Whisk egg yolks, sugar and custard powder in medium bowl until combined, gradually whisk in hot milk mixture. Add chocolate, stir until melted; stir in liqueur. Pour mixture into 20cm x 30cm lamington pan, cover; freeze until ice-cream is almost set.

3   Chop ice-cream roughly, beat in large bowl with electric mixer, or process, until smooth. Reserve 1 tablespoon of the chopped honeycomb; stir remaining chocolate honeycomb into ice-cream. Spoon ice-cream into prepared dishes, smooth top, tap gently on bench to remove air bubbles. Enclose dishes in plastic wrap; freeze until firm.

4   Finely chop reserved chocolate honeycomb. Spread melted chocolate evenly over 2 sheets of baking paper, each about 26cm x 28cm; sprinkle reserved honeycomb evenly over chocolate, leave to set.

5   Carefully remove chocolate from paper, break into long wedges, measuring about 3cm x 13cm.

6   Turn ice-cream onto plates, remove wrap, gently press chocolate wedges around sides. Serve immediately.

preparation time 40 minutes
(plus freezing time)
cooking time 5 minutes
serves 6

raspberry ice-blocks

1 cup (150g) frozen raspberries
⅓ cup (55g) icing sugar
1 cup (250ml) sparkling mineral water

1 Heat raspberries and icing sugar in small saucepan over low heat, stirring occasionally, about 5 minutes or until raspberries soften. Using back of large spoon, push raspberry mixture through sieve into medium heatproof jug; discard seeds.
2 Stir mineral water into jug. Pour mixture into six ¼ cup (60ml) ice-block moulds. Press lids on firmly; freeze 6 hours or overnight.

preparation time 10 minutes (plus freezing time)
cooking time 5 minutes
makes 6
note To remove ice-blocks from moulds, dip into hot water for a few seconds, loosen lids and squeeze sides of moulds – the ice-blocks should slide out easily. If you like, insert ice-block sticks into ice-blocks before freezing.

dried apricots in cardamom syrup with pistachio ice-cream

Ice-cream can be made several days ahead. Apricot mixture can be made a day ahead.

1 litre vanilla ice-cream, softened
⅔ cup (100g) coarsely chopped pistachios, roasted lightly
1⅔ cups (250g) dried apricots
2 cups (500ml) boiling water
¼ cup (55g) caster sugar
3 cardamom pods
1 cinnamon stick

1 Combine ice-cream and nuts in medium bowl; mix well. Divide ice-cream mixture among eight x ½-cup (125ml) moulds. Cover; freeze overnight or until ice-cream is firm.
2 Combine apricots and the boiling water in medium saucepan; stand 30 minutes.
3 Add sugar, cardamom and cinnamon to apricots; bring to the boil. Reduce heat; simmer, uncovered, about 10 minutes or until syrup is reduced by half. Cool 10 minutes.
4 Wipe ice-cream moulds with hot damp cloth and turn out onto serving plates. Serve with apricots and a little of the cardamom syrup.

preparation time 15 minutes
(plus freezing and standing time)
cooking time 15 minutes
serves 8

rhubarb crumble ice-cream

This recipe can be made 1 week in advance.

2 cups (220g) chopped rhubarb
2 tablespoons brown sugar
2 litres vanilla ice-cream, softened slightly
125g ginger nut biscuits, chopped coarsely

1 Line 14cm x 21cm loaf pan with plastic wrap.
2 Cook rhubarb and sugar in large heavy-based saucepan,
covered, about 5 minutes or until rhubarb is almost tender.
Reduce heat; simmer, uncovered, about 5 minutes or until
rhubarb softens but retains shape. Cool.
3 Place ice-cream in large bowl; break up slightly. Gently swirl
in biscuits and rhubarb mixture.
4 Pour ice-cream mixture into prepared pan. Cover; freeze
3 hours or until firm.

preparation time 10 minutes (plus freezing time)
cooking time 10 minutes
serves 8

glossary

almonds a flat, pointy-ended nut with a pitted brown shell enclosing a creamy white kernel that is covered by a brown skin.

blanched whole nuts with brown skins removed.

flaked paper-thin slices.

meal also known as finely ground almonds; almonds are powdered to a flour-like texture and used in baking or as a thickening agent.

vienna toffee-coated almonds.

biscuits

ginger nut a plain biscuit made with golden syrup and ginger.

lattice flaky pastry biscuits made from flour, oil, sugar and milk powder.

blood orange a virtually seedless citrus fruit with blood-red rind and flesh; it has a sweet, non-acidic pulp and its juice has slight strawberry or raspberry overtones.

butter use salted or unsalted (sweet) butter; 125g is equal to one stick (4 ounces) of butter.

buttermilk originally the term given to the slightly sour liquid left after butter was churned from cream, today it is commercially made similarly to yogurt. Sold alongside all fresh milk products in supermarkets. Despite the implication of its name, it is low in fat.

cardamom purchased in pod, seed or ground form. A member of the ginger family, it has an aromatic, sweetly rich flavour and is one of the world's most expensive spices.

chocolate

dark eating also known as semi-sweet or luxury chocolate; made of a high percentage of cocoa liquor and cocoa butter, and a little added sugar.

chocolate hazelnut spread a thick smooth paste that's made from chocolate and hazelnuts. We use Nutella; in its original form, it was first created in the 1940s. At the time, cocoa was in short supply because of rationing due to World War II, and chocolate supply was very limited, so hazelnuts, which were plentiful at the time, were used to extend the chocolate supply. It is available from supermarkets.

milk most popular eating chocolate, mild and very sweet; similar in make-up to dark with the difference being the addition of milk solids.

white eating contains no cocoa solids but derives its sweet flavour from cocoa butter. Very sensitive to heat so watch carefully if melting.

cinnamon stick dried inner bark of the shoots of the cinnamon tree; available in stick (quill) or ground form.

coconut, shredded thin strips of dried coconut.

coffee-flavoured liqueur we use Kahlúa or Tia Maria.

cream we used fresh cream, also known as pure cream and pouring cream unless otherwise stated. It has no additives, unlike commercially thickened cream. Minimum fat content 35%.

sour a thick commercially-cultured soured cream. Minimum fat content 35%.

thickened a whipping cream containing a thickener. Minimum fat content 35%.

crème de cacao chocolate-flavoured liqueur.

crème de framboise raspberry-flavoured liqueur.

Crunchie bar a honeycomb bar coated in chocolate.

eggs some recipes may call for raw or barely cooked eggs; exercise caution if there is a salmonella problem in your area.

evaporated milk this is an unsweetened canned milk from which water has been extracted by evaporation.

flour, plain an all-purpose flour made from wheat.

gelatine we used powdered gelatine. It is also available in sheet form, known as leaf gelatine.

ginger, crystallised fresh ginger root, cubed and preserved in syrup then coated in sugar.

hazelnuts also known as filberts; plump, grape-size, rich, sweet nut having a brown inedible skin that is removed by rubbing heated nuts together vigorously in a tea-towel.

jelly crystals also known as jello. A granulated, powdered mixture of gelatine, sweetener and artificial fruit flavouring that's used to make a moulded, translucent, quivering dessert.

kiwifruit also known as chinese gooseberry. Has a brown, somewhat hairy skin and bright-green or yellow flesh with a unique sweet-tart flavour.

limoncello a digestive (an alcoholic drink that is used to stimulate or assist digestion; usually taken at the end of the meal). Made from the peel only of fragrant lemons. The peels are steeped in a good-quality clear alcohol then diluted with sugar and water.

lollies a confectionery also known as sweets or candy.

pavlova shells (meringue nests, pavlova nests) small crisp meringue shells (or nests) available from most supermarkets.

peanut brittle peanuts coated in a hard toffee coating; available from confectionery stores and some supermarkets.

peanut butter peanuts that have been ground to a paste; available in crunchy and smooth varieties.

pecans native to the United States but now grown locally; a rich, golden-brown, buttery nut.

pistachio pale green, delicately flavoured nut inside hard off-white shells. To peel, soak shelled nuts in boiling water for about 5 minutes, drain, then pat dry with absorbent paper. Rub skins with cloth to peel.

rhubarb has thick, celery-like stalks that can reach up to 60cm long; the stalks are the only edible portion of the plant – the leaves contain a toxic substance. Though rhubarb is generally eaten as a fruit, it is a vegetable. Also available frozen from most supermarkets.

rocky road a confectionery containing a mixture of marshmallows and peanuts covered in chocolate.

Snickers bar a confectionery made of a peanut butter nougat topped with roasted peanuts and caramel, and covered with milk chocolate.

sorbet a frozen dessert made with fruit juice or another flavoring, a sweetener (usually sugar), and beaten egg whites, which prevent the formation of large ice crystals.

sugar
  brown an extremely soft, finely granulated sugar retaining molasses for its characteristic colour and flavour.
  caster also known as superfine or finely granulated table sugar.
  icing also known as confectioners' sugar or powdered sugar; granulated sugar crushed together with a small amount (about 3%) of added cornflour.
  white a coarsely granulated table sugar; also known as crystal sugar.

vanilla
  bean dried long, thin pod from a tropical golden orchid grown in Central and South America and Tahiti; the minuscule black seeds inside the bean pod are used to impart a luscious vanilla flavour in baking and desserts.
  bean paste a unique blend of concentrated pure vanilla extract and vanilla beans (including seeds) in an all-natural sugar syrup.
  extract vanilla beans that have been submerged in alcohol. Vanilla essence is not a suitable substitute.

walnuts encased in a grooved, light-brown shell, this nut is rich, flavourful and high in fat and, therefore, should be stored in the refrigerator or freezer.

61

conversion chart

MEASURES

One Australian metric measuring cup holds approximately 250ml, one Australian metric tablespoon holds 20ml, one Australian metric teaspoon holds 5ml.

The difference between one country's measuring cups and another's is within a 2- or 3-teaspoon variance, and will not affect your cooking results. North America, New Zealand and the United Kingdom use a 15ml tablespoon. All cup and spoon measurements are level. The most accurate way of measuring dry ingredients is to weigh them. When measuring liquids, use a clear glass or plastic jug with metric markings.

We use large eggs with an average weight of 60g.

DRY MEASURES

METRIC	IMPERIAL
15g	½oz
30g	1oz
60g	2oz
90g	3oz
125g	4oz (¼lb)
155g	5oz
185g	6oz
220g	7oz
250g	8oz (½lb)
280g	9oz
315g	10oz
345g	11oz
375g	12oz (¾lb)
410g	13oz
440g	14oz
470g	15oz
500g	16oz (1lb)
750g	24oz (1½lb)
1kg	32oz (2lb)

LIQUID MEASURES

METRIC	IMPERIAL
30ml	1 fluid oz
60ml	2 fluid oz
100ml	3 fluid oz
125ml	4 fluid oz
150ml	5 fluid oz (¼ pint/1 gill)
190ml	6 fluid oz
250ml	8 fluid oz
300ml	10 fluid oz (½ pint)
500ml	16 fluid oz
600ml	20 fluid oz (1 pint)
1000ml (1 litre)	1¾ pints

LENGTH MEASURES

METRIC	IMPERIAL
3mm	⅛in
6mm	¼in
1cm	½in
2cm	¾in
2.5cm	1in
5cm	2in
6cm	2½in
8cm	3in
10cm	4in
13cm	5in
15cm	6in
18cm	7in
20cm	8in
23cm	9in
25cm	10in
28cm	11in
30cm	12in (1ft)

OVEN TEMPERATURES

These oven temperatures are only a guide for conventional ovens. For fan-forced ovens, check the manufacturer's manual.

	°C (CELSIUS)	°F (FAHRENHEIT)	GAS MARK
Very slow	120	250	½
Slow	150	275-300	1-2
Moderately slow	160	325	3
Moderate	180	350-375	4-5
Moderately hot	200	400	6
Hot	220	425-450	7-8
Very hot	240	475	9

index

ACP BOOKS

General manager Christine Whiston
Editorial director Susan Tomnay
Creative director Hieu Chi Nguyen
Designer Melissa Deare
Senior editor Wendy Bryant
Food director Pamela Clark
Test Kitchen manager Belinda Farlow
Director of sales Brian Cearnes
Marketing manager Bridget Cody
Marketing & promotions assistant Xanthe Roberts
Senior business analyst Rebecca Varela
Operations manager David Scotto
Production manager Victoria Jefferys
European rights enquiries Laura Bamford
lbamford@acpuk.com

ACP Books are published by ACP Magazines
a division of PBL Media Pty Limited
Publishing director, Women's lifestyle Pat Ingram
Director of sales, Women's lifestyle Lynette Phillips
Commercial manager, Women's lifestyle Seymour Cohen
Marketing director, Women's lifestyle Matthew Dominello
Research director, Women's lifestyle Justin Stone
PBL Media, Chief Executive Officer Ian Law

Cover Brownie ice-cream stack with hot mocha fudge sauce, page 25
Photographer Ian Wallace
Stylist Sarah O'Brien
Food preparation Alison Webb
Back cover at left, Quick mango ice-cream, page 5;
at right, Mango vanilla frozen yogurt swirls, page 49.

Produced by ACP Books, Sydney.
Published by ACP Books,
a division of ACP Magazines Ltd,
54 Park St, Sydney; GPO Box 4088,
Sydney, NSW 2001
phone (02) 9282 8618 fax (02) 9267 9438.
acpbooks@acpmagazines.com.au
www.acpbooks.com.au
Printed by Dai Nippon in Korea.
Australia Distributed by Network Services, phone +61 2 9282 8777; fax +61 2 9264 3278
networkweb@networkservicescompany.com.au
United Kingdom Distributed by Australian Consolidated Press (UK),
phone (01604) 642 200; fax (01604) 642 300; books@acpuk.com
New Zealand Distributed by Netlink Distribution Company, phone (9) 366 9966; ask@ndc.co.nz
South Africa Distributed by PSD Promotions, phone (27 11) 392 6065/6/7; fax (27 11) 392 6079/80; orders@psdprom.co.za
Canada Distributed by Publishers Group Canada phone (800) 663 5714; fax (800) 565 3770; service@raincoast.com

A catalogue record for this book is available from the British Library.

ISBN 978 1 86396 884 3
© ACP Magazines Ltd 2009
ABN 18 053 273 546

Send recipe enquiries to:
recipeenquiries@acpmagazines.com.au